140 Life Lessons
I Wish I Knew at 20

#FSB140

D1290008

Fatimah S. Baeshen

To the classes of 2020, 2021, 2022 and beyond;
because humanity is in your hands.

To Minh Ly;
for always surfacing unexpectedly when I need it most.
Thank you.

And, to Hodi;
because 23 years ago; I promised you.

EPILOGUE:

When I hit 40 a few years ago — a light bulb went off. Self-acceptance "dropped on me like a ton of bricks," as I heard Jada Pinkett Smith once describe it. The clarity you gain is like crystal, and now at 42; I can't stop thinking — good God, why didn't anybody share life's lessons with me sooner. Is there some memo circulating, and I just didn't get cc'd? For the record: folks tried to copy me in intermittently along the way. But, I was too engrossed in youth and 'being independent' to listen. Of course, you can't cut corners in life — the whole point is to live it: good, bad, ugly, or worst of all… indifferent. The wisdom comes through trial and error… ultimately, gained through experience.

Like many during this pandemic, I've taken the time and space to deeply reflect — to take stock of life. I'm grateful to be able to look back at my journey thus far, having sieved out the wisdom through the painstaking process of working through the fear and releasing the resentment (both still get triggered, but thankfully — much less often). This work is akin to an abbreviated version of a life textbook I wish I had at 20 years old. These are the 140 greatest, and hardest, lessons I learned along the way.

I am not a psychologist, but I've delved into my own depths, and let me just say that the hardest thing I have ever had to do was confront myself. We can be inherently egotistical and too prideful to be open about struggles. We are open about success, but we tend to hide struggle — myself especially (a huge shout out here to Brene´ Brown's works on shame and the power of vulnerability, which lent me courage). I understand that knowing the lesson and having the discipline to apply it are two separate things. I'm no guru or expert nor am I perfect. I revisit this list frequently to remind myself. Like you, if you are reading this and it resonates — I too, will be figuring out the balance between wisdom and application. There is no cookie-cutter, linear process to healing. Life is messy, and we are unpredictable.

This list is not meant to be exhaustive, thematically sequential, neither cultural nor gender specific, or even conclusive. All I know is: this is what I know to be true for me thus far — after over 40 years of existence across many countries, cultures, states, and professions. I wish I had this script to refer to 20 years ago; as I was starting off. You may read this and think, 'well, duh,' which is, honestly, my greatest fear (so, there was a memo)! Or, you may say: 'nah, none of these really apply to me,' which is your call. Either way, I'm putting this out there in case this reference can help one random person get through a difficulty, make a choice, steer in a healthier direction, or just stop and think at any given point along the life path.

November 2020

FSB

Life Lesson #1:

Learn to dance with your demons. Accept every part of you—so you don't go around searching externally to be accepted.

Life Lesson #2:

Don't mistake chemistry for compatibility.

Life Lesson #3:

From the moment you start working, save at least 10% of whatever you make (George Samuel Clason). As your next egg grows—invest some; keep some liquid.

Life Lesson #4:

You don't have to know what you want to do with the rest of your life at 18, but you do have to go to class.

Life Lesson #5:

Learn religion but embrace spirituality—
believe in a Higher Source.

Life Lesson #6:

Cherish childhood friends.

Life Lesson #7:

Set healthy boundaries by learning to say no.

Life Lesson #8:

Prioritize yourself mind, body, and spirit. Feed all 5 of your senses daily. But, beware: garbage in; garbage out.

Life Lesson #9:

Wait tables and be a maid to learn service with both pride and humility.

Life Lesson #10:

Learn to acknowledge, sit with, and process your feelings. The only way out is through.

Life Lesson #11:

Don't mistake ego for confidence.

Life Lesson #12:

Don't mistake pride with dignity.

Life Lesson #13:

There are differences among: self-esteem, self-confidence, and self-assuredness—you need all 3. You might have to dig deep, but they all come from within.

Life Lesson #14:

Don't mistake dogmatism for conviction.

Life Lesson #15:

Don't be afraid to negotiate and ask for what you deserve, but don't mistake entitlement for experience.

Life Lesson #16:

Have friends from different walks of life, backgrounds, ethnicities, countries, religions, ages, genders, and sexual orientations.

Life Lesson #17:

Connect with others; don't attach.

Life Lesson #18:

Love—love is only love if it's in action.
You will get your heart broken, but love
anyway; even if it's from a distance.

Life Lesson #19:

Forgive—people will disappoint you. Forgive them anyway. But above all, forgive yourself.

P.S. Forgiveness doesn't mean re-engaging.

Life Lesson #20:

Everything in life comes to teach us a lesson. The more resistant we are—the harder the lessons become.

Life Lesson #21:

Don't mistake status for success. You will have to figure out what success means to you. Then be willing to hustle for it.

Life Lesson #22:

Nothing external validates who you are or your worth, e.g., numbers, people, letters, institutions. Neither will anything external make you content, e.g., luxury items, relationships, career. Validation and contentment are inside jobs.

Life Lesson #23:

Lose yourself to find yourself—try your hand at many things, especially earlier in life and career. So, you can sense what you are passionate about—then pursue it unapologetically.

Life Lesson #24:

Acknowledge and work through any trauma you have, then let it go. Sweeping it under the rug will only make it worse, and it will rear its ugly head throughout life across all spheres.

Life Lesson #25:

Don't let your struggles define you.

Life Lesson #26:

Treat others with decency and respect;
even if they don't deserve it.

Life Lesson #27:

Cut toxicity out of your life with a quickness. If it's confusing, draining, or causing you anxiety— cut it out immediately.

Life Lesson #28:

Enjoy your own company and get comfortable with going out alone. Be complete within yourself.

Life Lesson #29:

Build strong relationships with your siblings. They will be your closest family when your parents are gone.

Life Lesson #30:

Second to the connection you have with yourself; your relationship with your parents sets the stage for all other interactions in life. If childhood wasn't easy; learn to heal, forgive, and love your parents—even if that means from a distance or it takes time. Parents are humans without a manual. They did the best they could with what they knew at the time, which was likely passed down to them.

Life Lesson #31:

Meditate to quiet your mind.

Life Lesson #32:

Life is unfair, but you don't have to be.

Life Lesson #33:

Treat those who may seem "less educated, titled, etc." with more respect.

Life Lesson #34:

Laugh heartily from your stomach, even in public.

Life Lesson #35:

Stay in touch with your college bestie.

Life Lesson #36:

*Move daily—exercise, even
if it's just a stroll.*

Life Lesson #37:

Aim for interdependence;
not co-dependence.

Life Lesson #38:

Let go of outcomes—you can't control anything or anyone but yourself.

Life Lesson #39:

You are a spiritual being having a human experience. Don't neglect your soul.

Life Lesson #40:

Be consistent.

Life Lesson #41:

Age gracefully.

Life Lesson #42:

When people treat you badly, 99.9999%
of the time; it has nothing to do
with you and everything to do with
them. Don't take it personally.

Life Lesson #43:

Respond as opposed to react.

Life Lesson #44:

You attract what you are—if you are not happy with where you are or who is around you; work on yourself.

Life Lesson #45:

Don't follow societal norms just because you are expected to, i.e., marriage, house, kids, etc. And, don't let anyone or anything else define or narrate who you are. Only you get to do that. Be you.

Life Lesson #46:

Strive to be a better version of yourself—
you are your only competition.

Life Lesson #47:

Control your emotions and your thoughts, or they will control you.

Life Lesson #48:

Pick-up a constructive hobby or outlet so that you don't self-medicate with food, alcohol, drugs, etc. Also, learn to unwind without the use of a stimulant or sedative.

Life Lesson #49:

Don't be ashamed to ask for help.

Life Lesson #50:

Play—everyday, connect with your inner child. S/he is still in there.

Life Lesson #51:

Don't compare your journey to anyone else's. And, don't judge anyone else—external judgement is a mirror of how you view yourself.

Life Lesson #52:

*Believe in yourself and be
your biggest cheerleader.*

Life Lesson #53:

Believe in Karma — don't waste energy on revenge. Know that if you get shortchanged in any situation, the universe has a way of recalibrating to serve everyone what s/he deserves. Transversely, know that how you treat others eventually comes back to you — always.

Life Lesson #54:

Don't ever count yourself out. Apply and overreach, even if you don't think you'll qualify. Let the world turn you down, but always give yourself a chance.

Life Lesson #55:

*Keep your child-like enthusiasm
and curiosity. They make
you an eternal student.*

Life Lesson #56:

No matter what is happening; stay hopeful.

Life Lesson #57:

High school does not define you. If high school sucked for you — congrats! — your prime is ahead, and everyone else peaked early.

Life Lesson #58:

Always listen to both sides of the story.

Life Lesson #59:

Read information on the same topic from multiple sources. Even then, don't take it as gospel. Contextualize and pay as much attention to what is said; as to what is not mentioned. Then, form your own opinion.

Life Lesson #60:

After college — go work. Then go to graduate school. Then continue working.

Life Lesson #61:

Take a gap year and travel on a budget, even domestically.

Life Lesson #62:

Pay attention to signs from the universe and listen to your gut.

Life Lesson #63:

If you think the world is against you; remember the universe has your back — stay positive.

Life Lesson #64:

My formula for success:
good intentions + hard work — credit/
passion + consistency= SUCCESS

Life Lesson #65:

We are all struggling at various intervals and different gradations — be kind.

Life Lesson #66:

You can't choose the hand life deals you; always play your best. But, "you got to know when to hold 'em; know when to fold 'em; know when to walk away; know when to run;" — Kenny Rogers nailed it.

Life Lesson #67:

Loyalty is paramount — choose wisely. If your loyalty and effort are not reciprocated — that's usury.

Life Lesson #68:

The most valuable currency in life is time — not money. Forget the adage time is money. Time is energy — choose how and where you expend your time and energy. You can always make more money, but once you expend your time and energy — they are gone for good. Prioritize what matters.

Life Lesson #69:

Aspire to add value. Don't chase money, fame, or status — these can be by-products of pursuing your passion; but not the ultimate goal.

Life Lesson #70:

Never compromise your integrity;
your conscience will reward you.

Life Lesson #71:

*Always help others, but
don't be a door mat.*

Life Lesson #72:

Don't make decisions based out of fear. Instead, harness that energy and use it to propel yourself forward.

Life Lesson #73:

Ask questions.

Life Lesson #74:

Read the fine print before you sign.

Life Lesson #75:

You won't always get closure — move on anyway.

Life Lesson #76:

Be a reliable friend.

Life Lesson #77:

Do an internship.

Life Lesson #78:

Whatever you do, do it to the best of your ability—whether it's mopping or public speaking. Be so present and purposeful with the task at hand, that your absence is felt upon completion.

Life Lesson #79:

*Trust the process — let things
take their natural course.*

Life Lesson #80:

People change, so will you. Some will stay in your life; others will fall off. It's OK.

Life Lesson #81:

There are some conversations you just can't comeback from — it's OK.

Life Lesson #82:

Have mercy on yourself, so you
can have mercy on others.

Life Lesson #83:

Make time to dance.

Life Lesson #84:

You can always start over. Rebuild with the scrap material.

Life Lesson #85:

Try. If you don't succeed, don't regret failing — celebrate trying!

Life Lesson #86:

*Get comfortable with change. It
will be the only constant in life.*

Life Lesson #87:

"What is meant for you will reach you even if it's beneath two mountains, and what isn't meant for you, won't reach you even if it's between your two lips."

(reference disclaimer: have seen multiple sources for this; thus unsure of exact attribution — Middle Eastern and/or Islamic saying[s]).

Life Lesson #88:

Find a good dream interpreter.

Life Lesson #89:

*Seek the counsel of others but
make your own decision.*

Life Lesson #90:

Don't worry about what others think of you. Only your opinion of yourself matters. Judge yourself well — make sure the voice in your head is gentle with you.

Life Lesson #91:

Stay grounded.

Life Lesson #92:

*In public speaking, to calm your nerves,
look up at the room but don't make direct
eye contact with the audience members.*

Life Lesson #93:

Be in nature.

Life Lesson #94:

Take a trip alone.

Life Lesson #95:

Always dress-up and show-up;
especially for yourself.

Life Lesson #96:

Take Epsom Salt baths.

Life Lesson #97:

Pray.

Life Lesson #98:

Don't be apathetic — take a stance.

Life Lesson #99:

Balance is everything.

Life Lesson #100:

Be your own boss. Figure out what you are good at and what you're passionate about—then start your own business and fulfill your purpose.

Life Lesson #101:

*Read **The Old Testament** of the monotheistic traditions, **The Alchemist** by Paulo Coelho, and **The Prophet** by Khalil Gibran*

Life Lesson #102:

*Keep up with what is
happening in the world.*

Life Lesson #103:

But, don't watch too much news.

Life Lesson #104:

As above, so below—be aware
of the planetary alignments.

Life Lesson #105:

Know the atrocities of history,
so you don't repeat them.

Life Lesson #106:

"It matters not how strait the gate, how charged with punishments the scroll, I am the master of my fate, I am the captain of my soul," Invictus — William Ernest Henley.

Remember that.

Life Lesson #107:

Smile and stretch every day.

Life Lesson #108:

Don't label people—that lacks the effort to understand an individual's dimensions.

Life Lesson #109:

You are empowered to change your mind and direction without explanation. Give yourself permission to take chances.

Life Lesson #110:

Don't mistake control or attention for love. There is no ego in love.

Life Lesson #111:

"When you get; give."—Dr. Maya Angelou

Life Lesson #112:

Believe in miracles.

Life Lesson #113:

*Visit people in the hospital
and go to funerals.*

Life Lesson #114:

If you get a cold or flu—eat fruit and rub Vicks on the bottom of your feet.

Life Lesson #115:

Don't let compliments or criticism get inside of you.

Life Lesson #116:

Don't rush the stages of life; embrace each phase fully. You will miss it when it passes.

Life Lesson #117:

Know that when you are down,
there's only one way to go.

Life Lesson #118:

Know that when you are up—it's easy to fall.

Life Lesson #119:

*Watch all of 'The Godfather' movies.
"Leave the gun; take the Cannoli"—in
life; leave the resentment behind,
but take the lesson with you.*

Life Lesson #120:

You have the power to change the world. Know and believe that.

Life Lesson #121:

If you failed Algebra, it's OK—there's still hope.

Life Lesson #122:

File your taxes.

Life Lesson #123:

Listen more than you speak.

Life Lesson #124:

Learn to understand another person's opinion without accepting or agreeing with it—it's the only way to come to a mutual solution.

Life Lesson #125:

Apologize.

Life Lesson #126:

Once you've earned it, enjoying the finer things in life does not make you shallow; not appreciating or finding joy in the simple things—does.

Life Lesson #127:

Go to therapy.

Life Lesson #128:

Life can change in an instant. Don't take anything for granted. In the morning, wake with gratitude in your heart and on your tongue. In the evening, sleep with gratitude in your heart and on your tongue.

Life Lesson #129:

Find the thing that makes you you—and protect it ferociously.

Life Lesson #130:

Your greatest weakness and strength
are one and the same. Embrace it.

Life Lesson #131:

Like loyalty, focus is also paramount. Hone in on what you want out of life, instead of what you don't want. And, focus on yourself—in other words, mind your own business.

Life Lesson #132:

Vote.

Life Lesson #133:

Stay true to your morals and values,
but don't be self-righteous.

Life Lesson #134:

You are allowed to rest without guilt.

Life Lesson #135:

You deserve love, peace, and all good things—not because you are productive; not because you are perfect; not because you are smart. Simply because you exist.

Life Lesson #136:

The most important relationship you will have in life will be with yourself. Love yourself first. If you don't like aspects of yourself, evolve but know you will never achieve perfection.

Life Lesson #137:

To be successful, at anything—whether it's self-acceptance or your career—you gotta do the work.

Life Lesson #138:

Trust people's energies—if it feels off, it is.

Life Lesson #139:

Don't betray yourself—be true to you always. Stop being polite to others at your own expense.

Life Lesson #140:

Finally, when you falter (and, you will—it's OK): rest. But, get back up and keep on truckin'...

THANK YOU & ACKNOWLEDGEMENTS:

Fifi

Mommy, Daddy, Hesh, Hodi, Naj, Nat B, Andrew &Nono

Hera Zee

Lydia Paull-Flores

Ashley Luke

Hoossam Malek

Augustin Maldonado & Angel Borges

Dee Hobbs

Kate Putnam-Delaney & Tim Delaney

Claire Howorth

Suzanne Orlando

Anthony Scaramucci

Melis Malatani

Ian Kleinart

Eman Quoteh

Amanda Palomino

Clubhouse App & Founders

Book Baby Team

Joseph Llovesky

Mona Shahab

Thore

The City of Oxford

Lafayette County

The State of Mississippi

The Pandemic